Stareway To Spelling ®

A manual for reading and spelling the most used words

Keda Cowling Cert Ed and Kelsey Cowling BSc (Hons)

This book belongs to:-

....

....

First Published in 2002
Revised Edition 2006 by:-

Toe by Toe Ltd.

8 Green Road, Baildon, West Yorkshire BD17 5HL

ISBN 0-9541095-1-1

Contact Details

Toe by Toe Ltd.	Phone: 01274-588278 (helpline)
8 Green Road	01274-598807 (sales)
Baildon	The *Stareway to Spelling* website is at:
Shipley, West Yorkshire	www.toe-by-toe.co.uk
BD17 5HL United Kingdom	info@toe-by-toe.co.uk

Frank Cowling

Frank made a major contribution in helping us to develop this manual. We have much to thank him for.

GLOSSARY

MUW = The Most Used Words in the English language.

NEGATIVES = Words which students were unable to read or spell the last time they were tested.

SUS3 = Stare Underline Say 3 times (the reading procedure).

RAWS = Read Analyse Write Spell (the spelling procedure).

To help you understand the theory behind our methods, we recommend that you should read the following introduction. However, it is not absolutely necessary. If you prefer, you may turn to page 16 and begin with 'Before You Start'.

PREFACE FROM KEDA COWLING

For over 30 years I have tried one way after another to help people overcome severe spelling problems. In 1989 my son, Kelsey, came to work with me and - taking a similarly painstaking, analytical approach to my own - he finally developed a solution to the 'spelling problem' and his *RAWS* technique forms the foundation of this manual.

A basic tenet of any approach to spelling, however, is that we cannot spell words that we cannot read. In fact a word has to be read many times to get its imprint - especially the correct placement of letters - in the mind's eye. Therefore, reading exercises always precede spelling lessons as we progress through the 300 *Most Used Words* (*MUW*) which make up approximately three quarters of all the text we read. Unfortunately, many of these words are spelt non-phonetically and thus pose particular problems for a student with weak image recall. Anyone who has used the reading manual, *Toe By Toe*, will be aware that I am a firm believer in phonics as the key to helping people with reading difficulties. A child without reading difficulties can get by with very little formal phonics teaching, but a child <u>with</u> reading difficulties will rarely get above a reading age of 9 without an intensive study of phonics.

Words spelt non-phonetically, however, require a *Look and Say* approach. Please note that my *Look and Say* methods are not the run of the mill approach this term usually implies. I have called it my *SUS3* technique and we have found that a combination of this and Kelsey's *RAWS* technique produces the optimum results. Complete instructions for these techniques are provided, as and when required, throughout the manual.

After completing this manual, students will be able to read <u>and</u> spell the 300 *MUW*. They will then have the confidence to put pen to paper without fear of ridicule and - with the assistance of spell checkers - be able to produce legible, coherent writing for whatever purpose. A glance at our *Before* and *After* example pages will clearly show the effectiveness of our approach.

Finally, I have to say that children who learn to read and spell without difficulty will be able to manage perfectly well without this book - they simply don't need it. These children will form part of the great majority of the population who don't have to be taught, and manage with just a touch of phonics. In fact they can justifiably claim that they have never been <u>taught</u> how to read and spell.

Keda Cowling, 2002

Stareway To Spelling has been written for people (both children and adults) who have serious problems with literacy. It focuses on the *MUW* in the English language and is designed to help students who struggle to spell - and sometimes to read - these words. For the most part this group involves primary school children though it also includes a significant proportion of secondary school pupils and adults. We maintain that many of these people are - to some extent at least - affected by dyslexia which, even in this more enlightened age, often remains undiagnosed.

It is important to realise that people may be severely, moderately or slightly dyslexic. The extent of the problem can often be assessed by the weakness of their 'image recall' of symbolic information. They struggle to 'decode' words when reading and to retrieve and 'encode' words when writing and spelling. In effect, 'sight' and 'sound' do not work well together and there is only a weak connection between the two areas. These neural pathways are not well established so the correct choice of letters and their placement does not come easily. If the conventional spelling of a word is phonetically consistent, they may have no difficulty as it can be written as it sounds. Thus, they would have no problem spelling words like *not* or *can*. However, they may spell a word such as 'said': *sed.* They may have seen the word many times but - due to their weak image recall - they can only rely on sound to help them reproduce it.

In contrast, for a good speller, the connections between sight and sound are well developed. The neural pathways between the areas of the brain processing these senses are strong so, when writing a particular word, they can visualise the shapes and relative positions of the letters clearly. Indeed, if good spellers are unsure of the spelling of a particular word, they may well write out various versions to see which *looks* right.

This manual is designed to ensure that students can read and spell the 300 *MUW* quickly, confidently and accurately. In our classroom we regularly come across children who struggle with lists of spellings to learn for a particular school test. Ludicrously, these lists will often contain words such as *miscellaneous* or *technique* when children may still be struggling with *use* and *what*. Unless the words are phonetic, they may even find it difficult to read them. Even if they can reproduce the words in the list successfully, the words are not established in the long-term memory and are soon forgotten. If the student has to write the same words in 'sentence flow' they are often spelt incorrectly. Again, this is because the pathway between sight and sound has not been strengthened sufficiently. Don't worry if this seems confusing. All that is necessary is for the tutor to follow the instructions carefully. These methods are the result of many years of systematic development in our classroom and - that alone - guarantees results.

Why Spelling Doesn't Matter

It is an unfortunate fact that, in our culture, literacy skills are often regarded as the benchmark for intelligence. However, we maintain that it is a serious mistake to equate poor spelling with a lack of 'intelligence' in this way. Good spellers simply have an innate ability to process symbolic information and to remember the 'shape' of words easily but that does not make them particularly intelligent. Invariably, they have learned to read and spell with little conscious effort - regardless of any strategies their teachers may have used. Other people, however, do not have this innate ability. They do not remember how to spell high frequency words easily and are often labelled slow - or even lazy - by people who simply cannot understand why these children appear to struggle so much with reading and spelling. Most people have learned to read and spell so easily that they cannot even remember the process and thus find it difficult to understand how others may find the attainment of functional literacy such a hard task. It is worth remembering, moreover, that people with weak literacy skills are often highly skilled and efficient in fields that do not require the processing and manipulation of symbols.

Parents and teachers often complain that they can get their students over the reading hurdle but poor spelling remains an intractable problem. Indeed, in Britain, the debate over poor spelling skills has intensified with the Government sending out long lists of words (often difficult and phonetically inconsistent) to schools that <u>all</u> students are expected to be able to spell. Firstly, we have to say that - providing the words are actually intelligible - poor spelling simply should not be a matter of great concern. Indeed, standardised spelling only came in with the advent of typesetting when it was the typesetters, rather than the actual writers, who decided what constituted 'correct' spelling. Furthermore, in the modern age, writing is increasingly done on computers with ever more sophisticated spell checkers at hand. Teachers and others should be encouraged to avoid making value judgements about their students' intelligence and potential on the basis of weak spelling and to concentrate more on content, ideas and imagination.

Why Spelling Does Matter

Having said all of the above, we do recognise that people - however unfairly - tend to judge a person's intelligence on their spelling. Perhaps understandably, employers will have such prejudicial attitudes when confronted with, what may seem to them, bizarre spelling mistakes. This is particularly the case with the *MUW*. People may not be surprised to see *sep<u>a</u>rate* incorrectly spelled as *sep<u>e</u>rate* but are shocked and may even be annoyed, to see *wich* rather than *which*. This tendency to be judgemental can make students self conscious and embarrassed about their spelling ability. They may feel disinclined to read and write and, as a consequence, do not develop the strategies necessary to improve their literacy skills.

This vicious circle becomes ever more damaging in an economy where service industries are increasingly replacing manufacturing as the main source of employment. In the past, the fact that people were functionally illiterate could go unnoticed if their employment did not require such skills. However, as economies and information technology continue to develop, such jobs are rapidly becoming scarcer. Those affected by dyslexia are often inhibited as writers and reluctant even to put pen to paper in many cases. Together with improving literacy skills, this manual is designed to increase the confidence and self esteem of such students. It does this by concentrating on the *MUW* in the English language. Many people are unaware that only 12 words make up one quarter of all those we read and write. 100 words form half and 300 account for approximately three quarters of all the words we use. Once students can read and spell these words confidently and accurately, it makes an enormous difference to their ability and inclination to express themselves in writing.

How Do We Assess Spelling?

There does not appear to be any generally accepted criteria for making an assessment of a student's spelling ability. Tests producing a particular spelling age (such as those designed by Schonell) remain popular and are perhaps useful in providing a rough guide. The nature of the English language, however, means that they are fundamentally flawed. There are simply too many ways of spelling the same sounds and correct 'guessing' will tend to distort test results. They are also open to abuse in the sense that there is a temptation for teachers to 'teach to the test'. Indeed, by using the spelling procedure outlined in this book, it would be possible to artificially inflate a student's spelling age by systematically teaching the relevant words. Of course, this would give a false indication of the student's ability.

Any well-structured, phonetic reading programme (we particularly recommend *Toe By Toe* and *Stride Ahead*) will have a positive effect on a student's spelling. Improvements in phonological awareness (such as the role of the *mute e*) will - to a limited extent - be reflected in a spelling age test. Also, the actual process of reading and word recognition will help to imprint the image of a word - whether phonetically correct or otherwise - in the student's memory. Be that as it may, most people affected by dyslexia will always remain likely to make spelling mistakes because of the large number of phonetically inconsistent words in the English language. In addition, we believe that most dyslexic students do not respond well to methods of teaching spelling which emphasise rules. Even if they can grasp the rule or pattern involved, they simply cannot internalise it and thus continue to produce unconventional combinations of letters to represent the sounds they hear.

It is our belief that such severe spelling problems cannot be solved though they can be circumvented. This book is not designed to increase a student's spelling age as measured in conventional tests. It is far better, in our view, to focus on high frequency words in order to boost confidence and reduce the embarrassment factor.

Why Do We Use Sentences To Evaluate Spelling?

It is frequently the case that students make errors while writing down dictated sentences yet the same errors are not evident when students are able to concentrate on individual words dictated from a list. Effectively the sentences help to highlight weaknesses which may not otherwise be evident. By systematically working on these *MUW*, we aim to provide students with a store of common words which they can read and spell confidently and accurately. When students write these sentences afterwards this will not only confirm their improvement, but they will also gain a welcome boost to their self-esteem. It seems to us that this is a far better approach than - an often futile - attempt to reach some arbitrary spelling age by the memorisation of lists of difficult, low frequency words.

WHO IS THIS BOOK FOR?

Students

Stareway To Spelling is primarily designed for children who have severe difficulties with spelling (and - sometimes - reading) high frequency words. In our experience, by the age of 7, children have developed the ability to associate sounds with symbols (phonological awareness). *Stareway To Spelling* therefore is suitable for children aged 7 and upwards. (NB: some younger children will have developed this ability at an earlier age. If this is the case, *Stareway To Spelling* can also be used with these children.) Other students with less severe or obvious literacy problems will also benefit from the book. Commonly, these students struggle with phonetically similar pairs of words (e.g. where / were…etc) and they are also likely to have blind spots with some of the *MUW* that we are targeting. The dictation sentences will prove useful in highlighting these **(see also, the Diagnostic Test on p.84)**.

Other people will also benefit from the manual. For example, those children and adults who are reasonably confident and accurate when dealing with the *MUW* but who may struggle with phonetically inconsistent, low frequency words. Students who need to learn particular words for an exam or wish to become more confident in spelling words relating to a particular subject will find the spelling procedure outlined in this book very useful. Dealing with particular words systematically, whilst following this spelling procedure, guarantees results.

Tutors

Teachers, support assistants and parents can all be tutors using *Stareway To Spelling*. Mentoring schemes such as 'buddy systems' will find the manual particularly useful. Special Educational Needs Co-ordinators (SENCOs) can also play a vital role either as tutors or through monitoring the progress of a number of students / tutors who are using the manual. Experience has shown that tutors need two particular qualities:-

1. *Patience:* Teaching someone with severe literacy problems to read and spell can be a frustrating experience. This is especially the case during the first few lessons if pupils struggle to match particular symbols (i.e. letters) with the sounds they represent. At this stage, the short-term memory can easily become overloaded. It is important to remember that pupils are usually trying hard and are not deliberately making spelling errors. A patient and systematic approach from the tutor is the key to success in the long term.

2. *Flexibility: Stareway To Spelling* is based upon many years of experience plus practical application and development in the classroom. Time and again this method has transformed the spelling ability of pupils with the severest difficulties. Consequently, we recommend that tutors follow the instructions as closely as possible. However, every pupil/teacher relationship is unique and students will have their own particular strengths and weaknesses. Tutors therefore, do need to be flexible. For example, in assessing when to introduce the *Paired Words* or judging when to drop a particular word from the spelling procedure to allow extra practice.

SPELLING COMPARISONS

Before embarking on *Stareway To Spelling*, we would like you to have some faith in our techniques. The following six pages contain typical examples of students' writing both before and after the application of the techniques outlined in this book. These are genuine copies of students' work and we believe they clearly illustrate the effectiveness of the *Stareway To Spelling* method. You may note that very few mistakes have been made after our tutoring - even in 'sentence flow'. You will also see, however, that the odd mistake does still occur and that there are places where the student has crossed out and made corrections. As we have pointed out previously, many children can spell words correctly when the word is isolated, but lose the image of the correct spelling when writing passages of text.

Once these 300 *MUW* have been mastered, we can reasonably claim that our students have become functionally literate. We are not expecting perfection - a small number of mistakes will usually still be evident. However, the strength of *Stareway To Spelling* is that it will highlight any remaining weaknesses and these can then be worked on if both tutor and student feel it is necessary. Please note also that our students are displaying a far greater maturity in their writing style. They have become less hesitant and much more accurate and fluent when spelling and writing.

In order to further illustrate the dramatic improvement in writing resulting from the application of our techniques, we have included opportunities for your students to write text - using controlled vocabulary - both before and after coaching. These *Before* examples precede the reading lists which introduce the vocabulary and should be dictated to the students before any remedial work begins. The *After* is dictated following completion of the appropriate spelling exercises. In this way tutors, parents - and the students themselves - will be able to see clearly the progress that has been made.

Actual example of a student's progress based on 1 - 50 *Most Used Words*.

Before

Before

> if one is ther you can get on o of the bus with it. Wich wone can wey yows for ol of it? How do thay do it the nansded. ther is whon in ech of ther Bacs But were ar they? When were they in the BuB as se sissa that it vas Big? Was it with you and Wath Is it for? can he have a werd with yor mum o not? wat is tish Be yor Bag and Wer is It from? At ech one he Put his on top Put thay ot eum of. I sed she can yows for of the wers.

After

After

> If one is there You can get on or off the bus with it. Which one can We use for all ot it? the man said. There is one in each of there bags but where are there they? when were they in there Pub as she said that it was big? Was it which with you and what is it for? ao can he have a word which with your mum or not? wat What is this by your bag and where is it from? At each one he Put his on top but they all came of. I said she can yse four ot the words.

Actual example of a student's progress based on 51 - 100 *Most Used Words*.

Before

> So you may wride to some of thees other men adout it feurst. menny more men woud like to go in time to see hear. coud could we see how is at Nondura tow. the pepol have deen so come and get some oyel for them. Mennny of them have deen a long time so he made him go feurst. go up and down if you like plot and them would you let the worta out. Has he deen over and did he get part ove my Worta. No was dun I call over pepel more them youe. yow will make m him look into it and find out how thees men are.

After

> So you may write to some of these other men about the first part. Many more men would like to go in time to see her. could we see who is at number 2 tow? the people have been so come and get some oil for them. Many of them had been a long time so he made him go fast. Go up and down if you like and then would you let the water out? Has he been over and did he get some of my water? N No way do I call other people more than you. You will make him look into it and find out how these men are.

Actual example of a student's progress based on 101 - 150 *Most Used Words*.

Before

> wrathe a gud sether ethr you folo me to woche.
> I hoeve you mind to shoe Him arod The plas ewe
> Were can go coget Theraindhe thome to teoc thow
> tele The boy Ihowand I dsowantto Heff Him I now his
> neme. Oan yiyaror bfor Theat awe vere soie
> cat Came to live wiv me. I fick The oadeemon
> wos affe The sem fiy fis in The sete. I
> seye it wel be gngt if Hb oley disebee mosee of
> aewe lisl pigs. I can guse see The lone thawe
> be hotmuch of it. wieny eny of ouw
> men mec a nuwe sad

After

> Write a good sentence before you follow me to
> work. I know you mean to show him around
> the place too. Where can I go to get the
> right form to take through? Tell the boy I
> know his name and I also want to help him.
> One year before that our very small cat came to
> live with me. I think the old man was after the
> same three things in the set. I say it will be
> great if he only gives back most of our
> little pigs. I can just see the line through but
> not much of it. Will any of our men make
> a new sound?

Actual example of a student's progress based on 151 - 200 *Most Used Words*.

Before

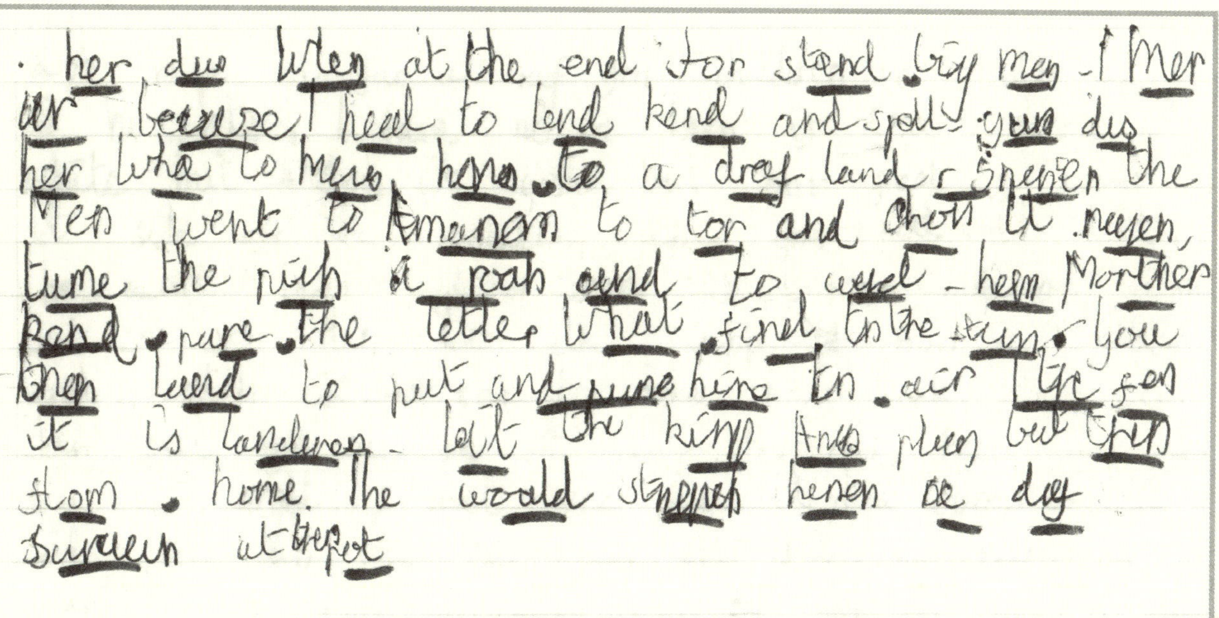

After

Actual example of a student's progress based on 201 - 250 *Most Used Words*.

Before

> It IS in pornt in Laif to owas Stat Schoot tgoth and ceepo dy on evrey group. Dont plant the tree undo or Blou the erth Said father. I thort you cud See the lit ohner the Sitey. he sor him boing to clos the lid wichofben opon the hed of yor ono cuntrey mu Set an exsampl at last. the St Toy will run for a waill if it Sems in gt ont to thos peo pe. the next Day he want a long and sat ＃ betwen This mthar and farth. neth oging tot Sunthing to the food if it is left. On papre life is hard for both of us duu set a exampel for a wail.

After

> It is important in life to always Start school together and keep an eye on every group. "Don't plant the tree under or below the earth" said father. I thought you could see the lights near the city. He saw him bigin to close the lid which was often open. The head over your own country might set an example at last. The story will run for a while if it seems important to those few people. The next day he went along and sat between his Mother and father. Never begin to add something to the food if it is left. On paper life is hard for both of us but set an example for a while.

Actual example of a student's progress based on 251 - 300 *Most Used Words*.

Before

> all mallu is farn in next for cauzed to ued untarl the car-loys. I hav idea in dany if the counls is wilthe but which is grown. put your fet in the riny at the sido of the mainnd ones you fen the neb. the youn inclain gdiw wated some two mishn Fallmen deut she sonn balri to toweck. sam for a swich and which haw far we cn cam for books. She whend to mee aen a naf toeat for own alla day and a niteke. lede us fatee it the conn in't red to the cau ah his body ale ram. he too her indamyr of a sons and pyun it tea meey befour it news leae. a ben it on the last was the shace be these

After

> A mile is far ~~deugh~~ enough for children to walk until the car leaves. I have no idea if the colour is white but ~~watch~~ watch it grow. Put your feet in the river at the side of the ~~maint~~ mountain once you feel the heate. The young indian ~~girl would~~ Sometimes miss her family but she soon began to talk. Stop for a while and watch how far he can carry four books. She went without enough to eat for almost a day and a night. Let us face it the colour is red so the cats on his body are real. He took her idea for a song and put it to ~~not~~ muisc before it was late. Above it on the list was the state by the sea

We strongly recommend that tutors follow the Lesson Guide (page 80) together with the Stareway to Spelling videos which are available on our website:

Tutors should familiarise themselves with the two appendices
supplied in the pockets in the inside back cover of the manual.

Appendix One

This consists of six sets of sentences which are to be dictated for students to write before working on the relevant words and again, afterwards, to show improvement and to highlight any remaining weaknesses.

Appendix Two

On the reverse of Appendix One is a template for two Spelling Forms. You need to make several photocopies of this template and cut them in half. When studying the RAWS procedure, it will be useful to refer to one of these forms to help understand what is required To help you get started, eight Spelling Forms have already been provided at the back of the manual.

Lesson planning

Our approach to spelling simply requires alternating between two procedures:-

- A tried and tested technique for learning spelling (the RAWS process).

- A marking procedure for controlling and recording the student's progress.

Stareway To Spelling is flexible in that it can be used successfully on a daily basis. However, for optimum results, tutors should aim to complete four lessons a week on separate days. Lessons should last for 15-25 minutes.

On the facing page, are the instructions for working through the manual. These are designed to guide both tutor and student through the system in a series of Six Steps. These Steps apply to groups of 50 words (out of the 300 MUW) though they can apply to blocks of 100 words - which often works better with stronger students.

*More information on **Stareway To Spelling,** including Frequently Asked Questions, can be found on our website:* **www.toe-by-toe.co.uk**

Stareway To Spelling deals with the 300 MUW in blocks of 50 words by following this sequence:-

STEP ONE Tutors take Appendix One and dictate sentences containing MUW1-50 for students to write in the appropriate *before* page of the manual (p.**18**-28).

STEP TWO Tutors ask students to *read* MUW1-50. Words they are unable to read are learned through the *SUS3* technique (p.30-37).

STEP THREE Tutors dictate MUW1-50 for students to *spell* on paper (p.39-41). Errors are written on the appropriate Control Page (p.**53**-59) together with any <u>additional</u> errors from *Step One*.

STEP FOUR Tutors choose 8 negatives* from the Control Page and teach students to spell them by following the RAWS process (p.42-45).

After a gap of <u>at least</u> 24 hours:-

STEP FIVE Any words <u>which have already been through RAWS</u> but do not yet have 5 consecutive ticks, should be tested on paper and marked with a tick or a dot on the Control Page (p.52-59)**. The negatives from *Step Four* should also be tested and marked (completing the RAWS process).

Steps Four and *Five* should be repeated until there are fewer than 8 negatives left on the Control Page before tutors return to *Step One* for MUW51-100 etc.

STEP SIX This final step should be taken when all the words on the Control Page have received five <u>consecutive</u> ticks. At this point, tutors take Appendix One and repeat the dictation for sentences containing MUW1-50 for students to write in the appropriate *after* page in order to make a comparison with their earlier efforts (p.**19**-29).

** Stronger students make fewer than 8 spelling errors when tested on MUW1-50. If this is the case, we recommend that the sequence of six steps should be applied to MUW1-100.*

***Remember: negatives need only go through RAWS <u>once</u> provided that afterwards, students are able to spell the words correctly on 5 consecutive occasions.*

Procedure for Dictation in the 'Before' Section

1) The tutor takes Appendix One and dictates the set of sentences based on 1 - 50 *MUW* for students to write in the *Before* section below.

2) Tutors should tell students when full stops, question marks and capital letters are necessary. Students should not dwell too long over the words. If they feel at all unsure, they should simply write the word 'as it sounds' and move on to the next one.

3) To minimise embarrassment avoid marking the sentences whilst students are watching.

Before

When these sentences are completed, return to page 17 and take *Step Two* on the *Stareway*.

Procedure for Dictation in the 'After' Section

1. Do <u>not</u> work on this page until you are ready to take *Step Six* (see page 17).
2. Cover the '*Before*' section on the facing page with paper or card.
3. Before starting, encourage students to apply the strategies they have been taught and to read back and check their own work.
4. The tutor again takes Appendix One and dictates the sentences based on 1 - 50 *MUW* in order to get a '*Before*' and '*After*' comparison.

After

Procedure for Dictation in the 'Before' Section

1) The tutor takes Appendix One and dictates the set of sentences based on 51 - 100 *MUW* for students to write in the *Before* section below.

2) Tutors should tell students when full stops, question marks and capital letters are necessary. Students should not dwell too long over the words. If they feel at all unsure, they should simply write the word 'as it sounds' and move on to the next one.

3) To minimise embarrassment avoid marking the sentences whilst students are watching.

Before

When these sentences are completed, return to page 17 and take *Step Two* on the *Stareway*.

Procedure for Dictation in the 'After' Section

1. Do <u>not</u> work on this page until you are ready to take *Step Six* (see page 17).

2. Cover the '*Before'* section on the facing page with paper or card.

3. Before starting, encourage students to apply the strategies they have been taught and to read back and check their own work.

4. The tutor again takes Appendix One and dictates the sentences based on 51 - 100 *MUW* in order to get a '*Before'* and '*After'* comparison.

After

Procedure for Dictation in the 'Before' Section

1) The tutor takes Appendix One and dictates the set of sentences based on 101 - 150 *MUW* for students to write in the *Before* section below.

2) Tutors should tell students when full stops, question marks and capital letters are necessary. Students should not dwell too long over the words. If they feel at all unsure, they should simply write the word 'as it sounds' and move on to the next one.

3) To minimise embarrassment avoid marking the sentences whilst students are watching.

Before

When these sentences are completed, return to page 17 and take *Step Two* on the *Stareway*.

Procedure for Dictation in the 'After' Section

1. Do <u>not</u> work on this page until you are ready to take *Step Six* (see page 17).
2. Cover the '*Before*' section on the facing page with paper or card.
3. Before starting, encourage students to apply the strategies they have been taught and to read back and check their own work.
4. The tutor again takes Appendix One and dictates the sentences based on 101 - 150 *MUW* in order to get a '*Before*' and '*After*' comparison.

After

Procedure for Dictation in the 'Before' Section

1) The tutor takes Appendix One and dictates the set of sentences based on 151 - 200 *MUW* for students to write in the *Before* section below.

2) Tutors should tell students when full stops, question marks and capital letters are necessary. Students should not dwell too long over the words. If they feel at all unsure, they should simply write the word 'as it sounds' and move on to the next one.

3) To minimise embarrassment avoid marking the sentences whilst students are watching.

Before

When these sentences are completed, return to page 17 and take *Step Two* on the *Stareway*.

Procedure for Dictation in the 'After' Section

1. Do <u>not</u> work on this page until you are ready to take *Step Six*. (see page 17).
2. Cover the *'Before'* section on the facing page with paper or card.
3. Before starting, encourage students to apply the strategies they have been taught and to read back and check their own work.
4. The tutor again takes Appendix One and dictates the sentences based on 151 - 200 *MUW* in order to get a *'Before'* and *'After'* comparison.

After

Procedure for Dictation in the 'Before' Section

1) The tutor takes Appendix One and dictates the set of sentences based on 201 - 250 *MUW* for students to write in the *Before* section below.

2) Tutors should tell students when full stops, question marks and capital letters are necessary. Students should not dwell too long over the words. If they feel at all unsure, they should simply write the word 'as it sounds' and move on to the next one.

3) To minimise embarrassment avoid marking the sentences whilst students are watching.

Before

When these sentences are completed, return to page 17 and take *Step Two* on the *Stareway*.

Procedure for Dictation in the 'After' Section

1. Do <u>not</u> work on this page until you are ready to take *Step Six*. (see page 17).

2. Cover the *'Before'* section on the facing page with paper or card.

3. Before starting, encourage students to apply the strategies they have been taught and to read back and check their own work.

4. The tutor again takes Appendix One and dictates the sentences based on 201 - 250 *MUW* in order to get a *'Before'* and *'After'* comparison.

After

Procedure for Dictation in the 'Before' Section

1) The tutor takes Appendix One and dictates the set of sentences based on 251 - 300 *MUW* for students to write in the *Before* section below.

2) Tutors should tell students when full stops, question marks and capital letters are necessary. Students should not dwell too long over the words. If they feel at all unsure, they should simply write the word 'as it sounds' and move on to the next one.

3) To minimise embarrassment avoid marking the sentences whilst students are watching.

Before

When these sentences are completed, return to page 17 and take *Step Two* on the *Stareway*.

Procedure for Dictation in the 'After' Section

1. Do <u>not</u> work on this page until you are ready to take *Step Six* (see page 17).

2. Cover the '*Before*' section on the facing page with paper or card.

3. Before starting, encourage students to apply the strategies they have been taught and to read back and check their own work.

4. The tutor again takes Appendix One and dictates the sentences based on 251 - 300 *MUW* in order to get a '*Before*' and '*After*' comparison.

After

Please study these instructions carefully before you begin

On the facing page you will see an authentic record of a particular student's performance. As you follow the *Reading Procedure,* glance across at the *Example Page* to ensure you fully understand the method.

The tutor writes the date at the top of the first column and works down the list asking the student to read every word. A tick or a dot (for negatives) is placed in the appropriate box in the grid.

The tutor then returns to the top and applies the **SUS3** technique to every <u>negative</u> in the list.

What does SUS3 technique mean?

It means <u>S</u>tare <u>U</u>nderline <u>S</u>ay <u>3</u> times.

SUS3 Technique

- Students are asked to stare intently at any negatives.
- Students must repeat the word aloud as the coach slowly tracks along the word with a finger.
- This is done <u>3 times</u> for each negative.
- It is essential that the students' eyes remain focused on the word throughout.
- Students should always follow the tracking of the tutor's finger and not blindly chant the sound of the word.
- This SUS3 technique is then repeated two more times. Each negative will then have been worked on a total of <u>9 times</u> in the session.

The **SUS3** grids at the bottom of the page require 3 ticks in the day's column. This is to check the number of times we have worked down the grid. <u>We never mark the grid again until the next day, even if the student appears to know the words</u> - note the different dates.

On the day of the second lesson, the whole process is repeated. On the third day, words that have two ticks can be ignored. You should work on the negatives only (i.e. those words that received a dot on either of the previous lessons).

Repeat on subsequent days until all negatives have gained three consecutive ticks. If no space remains on the grid, any remaining negatives should be ringed and returned to at every opportunity for more **SUS3** treatment (see **were** on the facing page).

Remember **SUS3**:   <u>S</u>tare <u>U</u>nderline <u>S</u>ay **3** times

M.U.W. 1-50 DATE:	9/9	10/9	11/9	12/9	16/9	17/9	18/9	
on	✓	✓						
had	✓	✓						
in	✓	✓						
but	✓	✓						
of	•	•	✓	✓	✓			
was	•	✓	✓	✓				
at	✓	✓						
word	✓	✓						
said	✓	•	✓	✓	✓			
with	•	✓	✓	✓				
are	•	✓	•	✓	✓	✓		
off	✓	✓						
if	✓	✓						
have	✓	✓						
what	•	•	✓	✓	✓			
each	•	•	•	✓	✓	✓		
they	•	✓	✓	✓				
she	✓	✓						
all	•	•	•	•	✓	✓	✓	
there	✓	✓						
is	✓	✓						
you	✓	✓						
by	•	✓	✓	✓				
or	✓	✓						
I	✓	✓						

M.U.W. 1-50 DATE:	9/9	10/9	11/9	12/9	16/9	17/9	18/9	19/9
the	✓	✓						
an	✓	✓						
for	✓	✓						
and	✓	✓						
be	•	✓	✓	✓				
do	•	•	✓	•	✓	✓	✓	
he	✓	✓						
that	✓	✓						
as	✓	✓						
your	•	✓	✓	✓				
we	✓	✓						
from	✓	✓						
their	•	•	✓	✓	✓			
were	•	•	✓	•	✓	✓	•	✓
not	✓	✓						
use	•	•	✓	•	•	✓	✓	✓
it	✓	✓						
how	•	✓	✓	✓				
this	✓	✓						
when	✓	✓						
his	✓	✓						
can	✓	✓						
to	✓	✓						
one	•	•	✓	•	✓	✓	✓	
which	•	•	✓	✓	✓			

SUS3 Grids	✓	✓	✓	✓				
Tick each time you **SUS3** the	✓	✓	✓	✓				
column.	✓	✓	✓	✓				

SUS3 Grids	✓	✓		✓	✓		✓	
Tick each time you **SUS3** the	✓	✓		✓	✓		✓	
column.	✓	✓		✓	✓		✓	

Remember SUS3:   <u>S</u>tare <u>U</u>nderline <u>S</u>ay **3** times

M.U.W. 1-50 DATE:							*M.U.W.* 1-50 DATE:						
on							the						
had							an						
in							for						
but							and						
of							be						
was							do						
at							he						
word							that						
said							as						
with							your						
are							we						
off							from						
if							their						
have							were						
what							not						
each							use						
they							it						
she							how						
all							this						
there							when						
is							his						
you							can						
by							to						
or							one						
I							which						

SUS3 Grids Tick each time you **SUS3** the column.							SUS3 Grids Tick each time you **SUS3** the column.						

Remember **SUS3**:   <u>S</u>tare <u>U</u>nderline <u>S</u>ay <u>3</u> times

M.U.W. 51-100 DATE:							
some							
her							
into							
could							
now							
than							
came							
did							
may							
over							
number							
make							
about							
so							
will							
then							
up							
way							
has							
would							
two							
go							
people							
down							
oil							

M.U.W. 51-100 DATE:							
made							
come							
been							
first							
no							
look							
call							
my							
see							
like							
more							
water							
get							
part							
day							
find							
long							
who							
time							
him							
many							
other							
these							
them							
out							

SUS3 Grids
Tick each time you **SUS3** the column.

SUS3 Grids
Tick each time you **SUS3** the column.

Remember **SUS3**:   <u>S</u>tare <u>U</u>nderline <u>S</u>ay **3** times

M.U.W. 101-150 DATE:									*M.U.W.* 101-150 DATE:								
little									show								
back									small								
me									old								
good									also								
say									too								
line									any								
same									where								
much									thing								
just									most								
after									take								
know									work								
year									name								
our									right								
help									form								
think									want								
give									through								
tell									live								
sentence									mean								
three									follow								
man									place								
before									very								
boy									sound								
set									great								
write									new								
around									only								

SUS3 Grids
Tick each time you **SUS3** the column.

SUS3 Grids
Tick each time you **SUS3** the column.

Remember **SUS3**:   <u>S</u>tare <u>U</u>nderline <u>S</u>ay **3** times

M.U.W. 151-200 DATE:							
ask							
England							
try							
again							
kind							
went							
large							
house							
should							
answer							
away							
spell							
change							
why							
even							
does							
hand							
because							
mother							
high							
still							
learn							
point							
animal							
listen							

M.U.W. 151-200 DATE:							
land							
men							
another							
turn							
air							
different							
move							
page							
us							
study							
picture							
here							
need							
such							
well							
read							
end							
must							
letter							
world							
play							
found							
home							
big							
put							

SUS3 Grids
Tick each time you **SUS3** the column.

SUS3 Grids
Tick each time you **SUS3** the column.

Remember **SUS3**:   <u>S</u>tare <u>U</u>nderline <u>S</u>ay <u>3</u> times

M.U.W. 201-250 DATE:									*M.U.W.* 201-250 DATE:								
seem									head								
open									along								
something									life								
father									school								
keep									every								
important									own								
paper									group								
next									food								
saw									under								
start									those								
add									often								
below									always								
might									close								
begin									thought								
example									last								
earth									near								
never									country								
plant									eye								
between									both								
hard									got								
together									few								
don't									story								
city									while								
tree									left								
light									run								

SUS3 Grids
Tick each time you **SUS3** the column.

SUS3 Grids
Tick each time you **SUS3** the column.

Remember **SUS3**: <u>S</u>tare <u>U</u>nderline <u>S</u>ay **3** times

M.U.W. 251-300 DATE:									*M.U.W.* 251-300 DATE:								
car									feet								
carry									began								
river									watch								
second									feel								
face									family								
sometimes									list								
almost									eat								
state									cut								
took									real								
sea									idea								
grow									stop								
walk									enough								
side									mountain								
above									young								
final									book								
far									mile								
children									music								
leave									late								
talk									white								
girl									song								
once									colour								
heat									soon								
night									miss								
until									without								
Europe									body								

SUS3 Grids
Tick each time you **SUS3** the column.

SUS3 Grids
Tick each time you **SUS3** the column.

We are now ready to start on the spelling exercises. You must follow these instructions carefully. They are designed to lead you through the procedure in a step-by-step manner, increasing your familiarity with the techniques involved. Intensive study of the entire procedure is not necessary, but this should help you to follow *Steps 3, 4 and 5* (page 17).

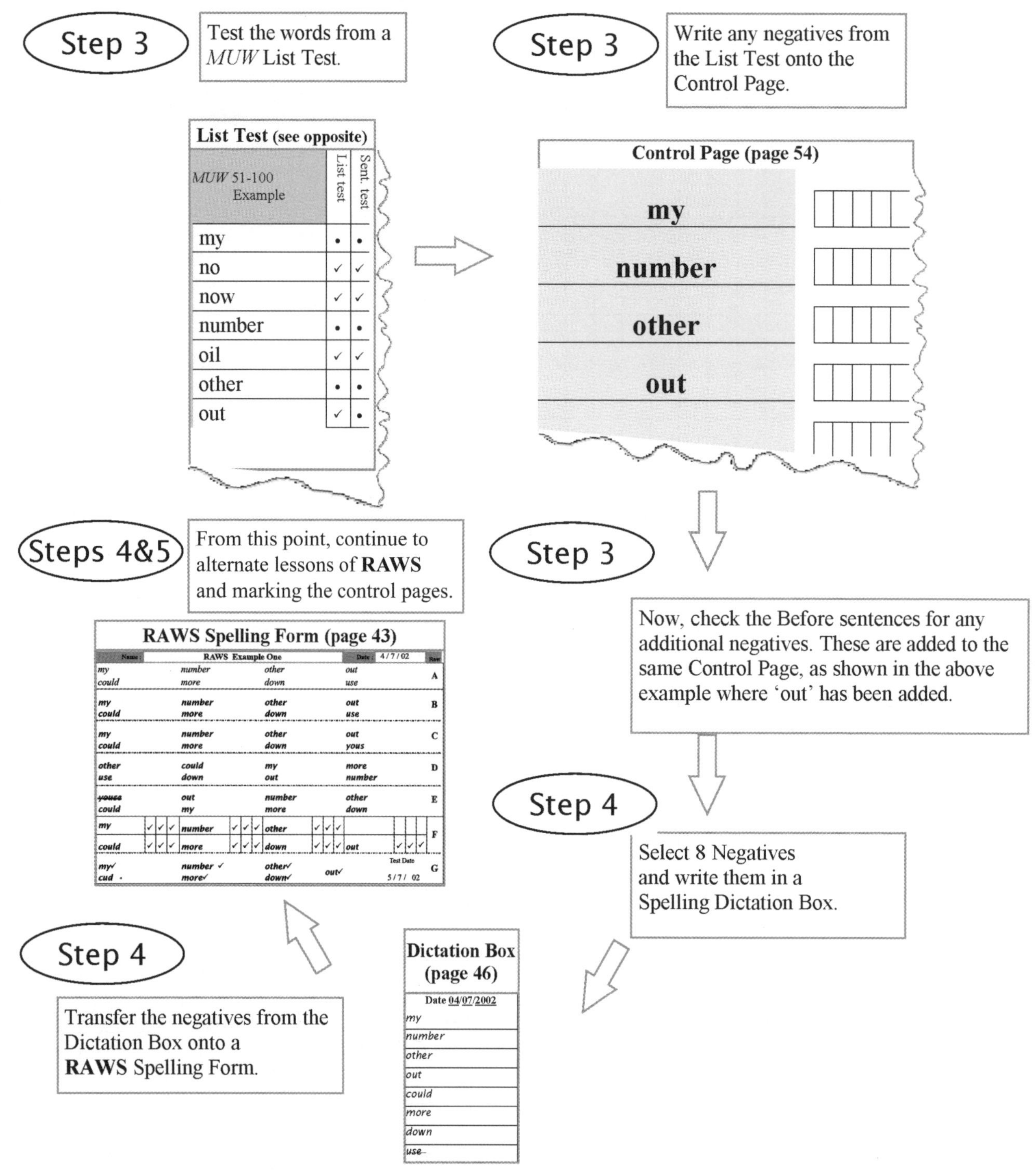

Begin by testing the lists of *Most Used Words* on the opposite page.

A) Dictate MUW 1-50 from the list for students to spell on paper. The *italicised* words can be spelt differently according to context. Therefore, you should offer a sentence containing the relevant word to see if the student makes the correct choice.

B) Mark the words in the *List Test* grid with a tick or a dot and write any negatives (words that have been spelt incorrectly) in the shaded area of the *Control Page* (p.53/54).

C) Check the 'Before' sentences (p.18/20) and mark the *Sentence Test* grids. Any <u>additional</u> negatives should be added to the same *Control Page*. Avoid adding the **bold** words (see Appendix One) as they are already on the *Control Page*.

D) Repeat the above for MUW 51-100 and continue overleaf with MUW 101-150 e.t.c as and when necessary.

MUW 1-50	List test	Sent test		*MUW* 1-50	List test	Sent test		*MUW* 51-100	List test	Sent test		*MUW* 51-100	List test	Sent test
1 all				23 it				51 about				75 my		
2 an				24 *not*				52 *been*				76 *no*		
3 and				25 on				53 call				77 now		
4 are				26 *one*				54 come				78 number		
5 as				27 or				55 could				79 oil		
6 at				28 said				56 day				80 other		
7 *be*				29 she				57 did				81 out		
8 but				30 that				58 down				82 over		
9 *by*				31 the				59 *find*				83 part		
10 came				32 they				60 first				84 people		
11 can				33 this				61 get				85 *see*		
12 do				34 to				62 go				86 so		
13 each				35 use				63 has				87 *some*		
14 from				36 was				64 her				88 than		
15 had				37 we				65 him				89 them		
16 have				38 what				66 into				90 then		
17 he				39 when				67 like				91 these		
18 his				40 *which*				68 long				92 time		
19 I				41 with				69 *look*				93 *two*		
20 if				42 word				70 *made*				94 up		
21 in				43 you				71 make				95 water		
22 is				44 your				72 many				96 *way*		
								73 may				97 will		
								74 *more*				98 *would*		

Paired Words (e.g. *were/where, off/of*) are omitted from these tests as they consistently cause problems. They have already been transferred to the *Control Page*.

A) Dictate MUW 101-150 from the list for students to spell on paper. The *italicised* words can be spelt differently according to context. Therefore, you should offer a sentence containing the relevant word to see if the student makes the correct choice.

B) Mark the words in the *List Test* grid with a tick or a dot and write any negatives in the shaded area of the *Control Page* (p.55/56).

C) Check the 'Before' sentences (p.22/24) and mark the *Sentence Test* grids. Any <u>additional</u> negatives should be added to the same *Control Page*. Avoid adding the **bold** words (see Appendix One) as they are already on the *Control Page*.

D) Repeat the above for MUW 151-200 and continue on the facing page with MUW 201-250 e.t.c as and when necessary.

MUW 101-150	List test	Sent. test		*MUW* 101-150	List test	Sent. test
101 after				125 old		
102 also				126 only		
103 any				127 *our*		
104 around				128 place		
105 back				129 same		
106 before				130 say		
107 boy				131 sentence		
108 follow				132 set		
109 form				133 show		
110 give				134 small		
111 good				135 sound		
112 *great*				136 take		
113 help				137 tell		
114 just				138 thing		
115 line				139 think		
116 little				140 three		
117 live				141 *through*		
118 man				142 *too*		
119 me				143 very		
120 mean				144 want		
121 most				145 work		
122 much				146 year		
123 name						
124 *new*						

MUW 151-200	List test	Sent. test		*MUW* 151-200	List test	Sent. test
151 again				176 listen		
152 air				177 men		
153 animal				178 mother		
154 another				179 move		
155 answer				180 must		
156 ask				181 *need*		
157 away				182 page		
158 because				183 picture		
159 big				184 play		
160 change				185 point		
161 different				186 put		
162 does				187 *read*		
163 end				188 should		
164 England				189 spell		
165 even				190 still		
166 found				191 study		
167 hand				192 such		
168 *high*				193 try		
169 home				194 turn		
170 house				195 us		
171 kind				196 well		
172 land				197 went		
173 large				198 why		
174 learn				199 world		
175 letter						

Paired Words have already been transferred to the *Control Page*.

A) Dictate MUW 201-250 from the list for students to spell on paper. The *italicised* words can be spelt differently according to context. Therefore, you should offer a sentence containing the relevant word to see if the student makes the correct choice.

B) Mark the words in the *List Test* grid with a tick or a dot and write any negatives in the shaded area of the *Control Page* (p.57/58).

C) Check the 'Before' sentences (p.26/28) and mark the *Sentence Test* grids. Any <u>additional</u> negatives should be added to the same *Control Page*. Avoid adding the **bold** words (see Appendix One) as they are already on the *Control Page*.

D) Repeat the above for MUW 251-300 as and when necessary.

MUW 201-250	List test	Sent. test		*MUW 201-250*	List test	Sent. test		*MUW 251-300*	List test	Sent. test		*MUW 251-300*	List test	Sent. test
201 add				226 left				251 above				276 list		
202 along				227 life				252 almost				277 mile		
203 always				228 light				253 began				278 miss		
204 begin				229 might				254 body				279 mountain		
205 below				230 near				255 *book*				280 music		
206 between				231 never				256 car				281 *night*		
207 both				232 next				257 carry				282 once		
208 city				233 often				258 children				283 *real*		
209 close				234 open				259 colour				284 river		
210 country				235 own				260 cut				285 *sea*		
211 don't				236 paper				261 eat				286 second		
212 earth				237 plant				262 enough				287 *side*		
213 every				238 run				263 Europe				288 sometimes		
214 example				239 saw				264 face				289 song		
215 *eye*				240 school				265 family				290 soon		
216 *father*				241 *seem*				266 far				291 state		
217 few				242 something				267 feel				292 stop		
218 food				243 start				268 *feet*				293 talk		
219 got				244 *story*				269 final				294 *took*		
220 group				245 those				270 girl				295 until		
221 hard				246 thought				271 grow				296 walk		
222 head				247 together				272 heat				297 watch		
223 important				248 tree				273 idea				298 white		
224 keep				249 under				274 late				299 without		
225 last				250 while				275 leave				300 young		

Paired Words have already been transferred to the *Control Page*.

What does RAWS Process mean?

Read   Read the words

Analyse   Analyse the words

Write   Write the words

Spell   Spell the words verbally

Row A   The tutor selects 8 words from a *Control Page* which have not been marked, or that have a dot in the last column before writing them on *Row A* of a *Spelling Form* and in a *Spelling Dictation Box* (p.46-51). The tutor confirms that the student can **R**ead the words.

Row B   Tutor and student **A**nalyse the words together using the Word Guides at the back of the manual (p.68-79).
Students then copy each word onto *Row B*.

Row C   The tutor checks the words and folds the form on the dotted line so that the words are hidden.
The tutor dictates the words from the *Spelling Dictation Box* for the student to **W**rite in *Row C*.
Allow the student to write all the words before checking for errors. If errors do occur follow the notes opposite.

Row D   Repeat the instructions for *Row C*.

Row E   Repeat the instructions for *Row C*.

Row F   The student copies the words onto *Row F*.
The tutor takes the form and, choosing the words at random, asks the student to **S**pell the words <u>verbally</u>. This is done 3 times with the tutor varying the order each time. 3 ticks are required for each word.

Row G   After a gap of <u>at least 24 hours,</u> fold the form on the dotted line and dictate the words for the student to write again. Transfer the results to the *Control Page*.

(Note: *Tutor handwriting style*, **Student handwriting style**)

Name :	Example One			Date : 4 / 7 / 02	Row
my *could*	*number* *more*	*other* *down*	*out* *use*		**A**
my **could**	**number** **more**	**other** **down**	**out** **use**		**B**
my **could**	**number** **more**	**other** **down**	**out** **yous**		**C**
other **use**	**could** **down**	**my** **out**	**more** **number**		**D**
~~**youse**~~ **could**	**out** **my**	**number** **more**	**other** **down**		**E**
my ✓ ✓ ✓ **could** ✓ ✓ ✓	**number** ✓ ✓ ✓ **more** ✓ ✓ ✓	**other** ✓ ✓ ✓ **down** ✓ ✓ ✓	**out** ✓ ✓ ✓		**F**
my ✓ **cud** •	**number** ✓ **more** ✓	**other** ✓ **down** ✓	**out** ✓	Test Date 5 / 7 / 02	**G**

How To Treat Errors

Errors
- <u>Wait until the *Row* has been completed</u>.
- Challenge the student to identify the mistakes.
- Once identified, use the *Word Guides* to repeat analysis of the negatives.
- The student should trace over the word on *Row A* with their finger whilst repeating it aloud. Do this 3 times. N.B. students should not pronounce each individual letter, but simply say the word as they hear it.

Repeated Errors
- Explain that more practice is required.
- Draw a line through the words, both on the form (see 'use' in the example above), and in the *Spelling Dictation Box*.
- Try to include them in the next spelling lesson.

Verbal Errors

If mistakes are made in *Row F*, apply the 'invisible writing' technique. This is where students verbally spell the word, letter by letter, whilst 'writing' with their finger on the desk.

If they can't do this, or seem unduly hesitant, then cross the words out and include them in the next **RAWS** lesson.

(Note: *Tutor handwriting style,* **Student handwriting style)**

Name :	Example Two			Date : 4 / 8 / 02	Row
small *thing*	*any* *kind*	*also* *sentence*	*before* *follow*		**A**
small **thing**	**any** **kind**	**also** **sentence**	**before** **follow**		**B**
small **thing**	**any** **kind**	**allso** **sentence**	**befor** **follow**		**C**
also **follow**	**thing** **sentence**	**smoll** **before**	**kind** **any**		**D**
follow **thing**	~~**befour**~~ **small**	**any** **kind**	~~**alsow**~~ **sentence**		**E**
small ✓ ✓ ✓ **any** ✓ ✓ ✓ **thing** ✓ ✓ ✓ **kind** ✓ ✓ ✓ **sentence** ✓ ✓ ✓ **follow** ✓ ✓ ✓					**F**
small ✓ **thing** ✓	**eny** • **kind** ✓	**sentens** •	**follow** ✓	Test Date 5 / 8 / 02	**G**

How To Treat Errors

Errors
- <u>Wait until the *Row* has been completed.</u>
- Challenge the student to identify the mistakes.
- Once identified, use the *Word Guides* to repeat analysis of the negatives.
- The student should trace over the word on *Row A* with their finger whilst repeating it aloud. Do this 3 times. N.B. students should not pronounce each individual letter, but simply say the word as they hear it.

Repeated Errors
- Explain that more practice is required.
- Draw a line through the words, both on the form (see 'also' and 'before' in the example above), and in the *Spelling Dictation Box*.
- Try to include them in the next spelling lesson.

Verbal Errors

If mistakes are made in *Row F*, apply the 'invisible writing' technique. This is where students verbally spell the word, letter by letter, whilst 'writing' with their finger on the desk.

If they can't do this, or seem unduly hesitant, then cross the words out and include them in the next **RAWS** lesson.

Name : Example Three (Before Starting RAWS Process)			Date : 4 / 9 / 02	Row
seem thought	something don't	important group	father while	A
				B
				C
				D
				E
				F
			Test Date	G

(Note: *Tutor handwriting style*, **Student handwriting style**)

Partially Completed RAWS Form

Name : Example Four			Date : 4 / 9 / 02	Row
seem thought	something don't	important group	father while	A
seem thought	something don't	important group	father while	B
seem thought	something don't	important group	farther while	C
important while	thought group	seem father	don't something	D
while thought	father seem	something don't	important group	E
seem ✓ ✓ ✓ thought •	something ✓ ✓ ✓ don't ✓ ✓ ✓	important ✓ ✓ ✓ group ✓ ✓ ✓	father ✓ ✓ ✓ while ✓ ✓ ✓	F
			Test Date	G

Spelling Dictation Boxes

These boxes form part of the RAWS process.

Date __/__/____	Date __/__/____	Date __/__/____	Date __/__/____

Date __/__/____	Date __/__/____	Date __/__/____	Date __/__/____

Date __/__/____	Date __/__/____	Date __/__/____	Date __/__/____

Date __/__/____	Date __/__/____	Date __/__/____	Date __/__/____

The tutor dictates the words to the student during a RAWS lesson.

Date ___/___/____	Date ___/___/____	Date ___/___/____	Date ___/___/____

Date ___/___/____	Date ___/___/____	Date ___/___/____	Date ___/___/____

Date ___/___/____	Date ___/___/____	Date ___/___/____	Date ___/___/____

Date ___/___/____	Date ___/___/____	Date ___/___/____	Date ___/___/____

These boxes form part of the RAWS process.

Date ___/___/____	Date ___/___/____	Date ___/___/____	Date ___/___/____

Date ___/___/____	Date ___/___/____	Date ___/___/____	Date ___/___/____

Date ___/___/____	Date ___/___/____	Date ___/___/____	Date ___/___/____

Date ___/___/____	Date ___/___/____	Date ___/___/____	Date ___/___/____

The tutor dictates the words to the student during a RAWS lesson.

Date ___/___/_____	Date ___/___/_____	Date ___/___/_____	Date ___/___/_____

Date ___/___/_____	Date ___/___/_____	Date ___/___/_____	Date ___/___/_____

Date ___/___/_____	Date ___/___/_____	Date ___/___/_____	Date ___/___/_____

Date ___/___/_____	Date ___/___/_____	Date ___/___/_____	Date ___/___/_____

These boxes form part of the RAWS process.

Date ___/___/____	Date ___/___/____	Date ___/___/____	Date ___/___/____

Date ___/___/____	Date ___/___/____	Date ___/___/____	Date ___/___/____

Date ___/___/____	Date ___/___/____	Date ___/___/____	Date ___/___/____

Date ___/___/____	Date ___/___/____	Date ___/___/____	Date ___/___/____

The tutor dictates the words to the student during a RAWS lesson.

Date ___/___/____	Date ___/___/____	Date ___/___/____	Date ___/___/____

Date ___/___/____	Date ___/___/____	Date ___/___/____	Date ___/___/____

Date ___/___/____	Date ___/___/____	Date ___/___/____	Date ___/___/____

Date ___/___/____	Date ___/___/____	Date ___/___/____	Date ___/___/____

Ignore the **bold** instructions below, until both tutor and student have become familiar with the RAWS process (*Step 4*) and marking the control page (*Step 5*).

The words printed in bold on the grids on the facing page are *paired words*. These need special attention. Once both tutor and student have become familiar with the marking procedure outlined below and the RAWS Process for teaching spelling, it is time to introduce the *paired words*. Before doing so, tutors will need to study the detailed instructions for *paired words* on pages 60-63.

When testing to see if students <u>can still spell words they have already been taught,</u> it is important to separate the *paired words* as much as possible. On paper, students should spell according to this sequence: column A words (e.g. *off, were* e.t.c…), the words on the grids (see *a, b and c* below) and finally, the column B words (e.g *of, where* e.t.c…).

A) Search through the grids for words which have not gained **five** consecutive ticks. Ask students to spell these words on paper and then mark on the *Control Page*. Remember to leave <u>at least</u> 24 hours between ticks.

B) Ignore words which have not yet been taught, or that received a dot on the previous attempt (negatives). These will be taken through the **RAWS** process. It is not unusual for some words to go through the process on several occasions.

C) After at least 24 hours have elapsed since the previous spelling lesson, complete the **RAWS** process - described on page 42 - by marking *Row G*. Transfer the *Row G* ticks or dots to the *Control Page.*

*Prepare for the **RAWS** process*

D) Take a new *Spelling Form* from the pocket at the back of the manual. Select 8 negatives from the *Control Page* and write them on *Row A* of the form and in a *Spelling Dictation Box* (p.46-51).

E) Before commencing the **RAWS** process we strongly recommend that you prepare by using the Word Guides (p.68-79) to study the selected words on the *Spelling Form*. Your main task when teaching spelling is to help the student **Analyse** the words during the **RAWS** process. By studying the Word Guide, you will be better prepared to pre-empt your student's mistakes. Discussing potential errors has proven invaluable in helping students to spell accurately.

A	B	Paired Words
off	of	
were	where	
their	there	
for	four	

After a word has received its first tick, wait at least 24 hours before asking your student to spell it again on paper. When all words have 5 <u>consecutive</u> ticks, see *Step Six* on page 17.

A	B	Paired Words
who	**how**	

After a word has received its first tick, wait at least 24 hours before asking your student to spell it again on paper. When all words have 5 <u>consecutive</u> ticks, see *Step Six* on page 17.

A	B	Paired Words
write	right	
know	now	

After a word has received its first tick, wait at least 24 hours before asking your student to spell it again on paper. When all words have 5 <u>consecutive</u> ticks, see *Step Six* on page 17.

Spelling 151 - 200 *MUW* Control Page

A	B	Paired Words
hear	**here**	

After a word has received its first tick, wait at least 24 hours before asking your student to spell it again on paper. When all words have 5 <u>consecutive</u> ticks, see *Step Six* on page 17.

A	B	Paired Words

After a word has received its first tick, wait at least 24 hours before asking your student to spell it again on paper. When all words have 5 <u>consecutive</u> ticks, see *Step Six* on page 17.

A	B	Paired Words

After a word has received its first tick, wait at least 24 hours before asking your student to spell it again on paper. When all words have 5 <u>consecutive</u> ticks, see *Step Six* on page 17.

A	B	Paired Words

After a word has received its first tick, wait at least 24 hours before asking your student to spell it again on paper. When all words have 5 <u>consecutive</u> ticks, see *Step Six* on page 17.

Teaching Guide

Use the following pages to help your student spell words which commonly cause the most problems. You can return to this guide whenever your student has difficulty spelling these words.

A major problem for weak spellers is a tendency to confuse particular word pairings. Experience and research involving hundreds of students over many years has indicated that the vast majority of students with weak literacy skills will have problems with most, if not all, of the eight word pairings in this guide. Consequently, each of them should be included in the **RAWS** procedure on at least one occasion. Of course, many of them will have to be included several times, so that the relevant strategies become automatic.

Homophones (words which sound the same but are spelt differently according to context e.g. *their/there, hear/here, for/four*) present major difficulties. Indeed, it is often the case that individuals who show few obvious problems in spelling high frequency words, will still have difficulties in this area. Aside from homophones, errors are regularly evident among other word pairings such as *who/how* and *off/of*. In our experience, confusion between *were* and *where,* is almost universal among students with literacy problems. This can manifest itself in both spelling and reading though, in the case of the latter, context will often help a student to differentiate between the words.

Individuals will also have their own particular weaknesses. If confusion between other word pairings does arise, then it is important to use the same procedure with these words. Tutors therefore, need to be alert to confusion between other words such as the following:

are / or	**be / by**	**other / over**	**us/use**	**one / won**
two / too	**want / what**	**these / this**	**far / fare**	**way / why**

Information about these words can be found in the *Word Guides* starting on page 68.

Changes to RAWS spelling procedure for Paired Words

Once both tutor and student have become familiar with the RAWS process, it is time to include some *Paired Words*. The basic procedure remains the same apart from the following alterations:-

Row A   The tutor ensures that 2 of the 8 target words are *Paired Words*.

Row B   Tutor and student **A**nalyse the *Paired Words* together using the *Paired Words Guide* (p.64-65). The other 6 negatives will be analysed as usual.

Row C   Dictate the words and then check them as normal.

Row D   Point out that <u>in these two rows,</u> some words may be repeated on more than one occasion. The aim is to prevent students from making assumptions about which word will follow: e.g. if they have already spelt **were**, they could

Row E   anticipate that **where** is coming next. We need students to develop a strategy for differentiating between these word pairings and only regular practice can help with this.

In **Rows D & E** of the form, the order in which students are asked to spell the *Paired Words* is very important. Students could be asked to spell the words in the order shown in the examples overleaf.

Example One

Row D		Row E	
1.	**were**	**1.**	**where**
2.	*many*	2.	*with*
3.	*with*	3.	*each*
4.	**were**	**4.**	**were**
5.	*great*	5.	*do*
6.	*each*	6.	*many*
7.	**where**	**7.**	**were**
8.	*have*	8.	*great*
9.	*do*	9.	*have*
10.	**where**	**10.**	**where**

By inserting two words in between each *paired word*, students are forced to 'think' about the difference between the words and apply any strategy or mnemonic which may help them. Regular practice helps to make this automatic. The order in which students are asked to spell the other words is of no particular significance. It is vital however, that tutors watch carefully when students spell the *paired words*, so that errors can be correctly identified. *Rows F* and *G* of the spelling form should be completed in the usual manner.

Example Two

Row D		Row E	
1.	**there**	**1.**	**their**
2.	*word*	2.	*does*
3.	*does*	3.	*through*
4.	**there**	**4.**	**there**
5.	*kind*	5.	*these*
6.	*which*	6.	*word*
7.	**their**	**7.**	**their**
8.	*through*	8.	*which*
9.	*these*	9.	*kind*
10.	**their**	**10.**	**their**

In the case of homophones, as in **Example Two**, tutors should offer a sentence that contains the relevant word and then watch carefully to ensure that students make the correct choice.

Remember: if they have made a mistake, students should be challenged to identify it once the row has been completed, rather than at the time.

(Note: *Tutor handwriting style*, **Student handwriting style**)

Name :	Example One			Date : 2 / 7 / 02	Row
were	*many*	*great*	*have*		**A**
where	*with*	*each*	*do*		
were	**many**	**great**	**have**		**B**
where	**with**	**each**	**do**		
do	**were**	**many**	**great**		**C**
where	**with**	**have**	**each**		
were	**many**	**with**	**were**	**great**	**D**
each	**where**	**have**	**do**	**where**	
where	**with**	**each**	**were**	**do**	**E**
many	**were**	**great**	**have**	**where**	
were ✓ ✓ ✓	**do** ✓ ✓ ✓	**many** ✓ ✓ ✓	**have** ✓ ✓ ✓		**F**
where ✓ ✓ ✓	**with** ✓ ✓ ✓	**each** ✓ ✓ ✓	**great** ✓ ✓ ✓		
where ✓	**each** ✓	**great** ✓	**have** ✓	Test Date	**G**
do ✓	**many** ✓	**with** ✓	**were** ✓	3 / 7 / 02	

Name :	Example Two			Date : 4 / 7 / 02	Row
there	*word*	*kind*	*through*		**A**
their	*does*	*which*	*these*		
there	**word**	**kind**	**through**		**B**
their	**does**	**which**	**these**		
these	**through**	**there**	**which**		**C**
kind	**word**	**does**	**their**		
there	**word**	**does**	**there**	**kind**	**D**
which	**their**	**through**	**these**	**their**	
their	**does**	**through**	**there**	**these**	**E**
word	**their**	**which**	**kind**	**their**	
their ✓ ✓ ✓	**does** ✓ ✓ ✓	**which** ✓ ✓ ✓	**through** ✓ ✓ ✓		**F**
there ✓ ✓ ✓	**word** ✓ ✓ ✓	**these** ✓ ✓ ✓	**kind** ✓ ✓ ✓		
does ✓	**there** ✓	**word** ✓	**these** ✓	Test Date	**G**
kind ✓	**throught** •	**which** ✓	**thier** •	5 / 7 / 02	

Tips for word analysis and mnemonics (memory aids)

The 4 sets of *Paired Words* below are homophones (words that sound the same, but are spelt differently according to context). Explain to students how they differ in **meaning**. The best way to establish that students have grasped the difference is to provide them with a few sentences containing one of the words and ask them to identify the relevant spelling on each occasion.

for / four

Point out the difference in meaning by providing a few examples. Students need to decide, in the context of a sentence, whether or not **for/four** is a number. Confusion here is complicated by **fore**. To reduce this, students should think about **four** <u>o</u>range <u>u</u>mbrellas (f - - r).

their / there

Problems with this homophone are extremely common. Explain to your student that **their** is possessive (i.e. it indicates 'belonging to') whilst **there** is not. The dot 'belongs to' the **i** in the<u>i</u>r. Also, to avoid common errors such as *thier* or *thire*, tell your student to write '**the**' first (<u>the</u>ir). Before commencing the spelling procedure, try to provide some examples of sentences containing **there/their** and ask your student to make the correct choice.

write / right

Explain that **right** is used on two frequent occasions:-
  i.e. for *right / wrong* and for *right / left* (r - - - - : <u>i</u>diots <u>g</u>ulp <u>h</u>ot <u>t</u>ea).
Write, on the other hand, is only used as in to ***write*** a letter (students should <u>*write*</u> the silent **w**).

hear / here

Explain to your student the difference in meaning. To ensure that this has been fully understood, try to provide a few sentences containing *hear/here* and challenge your student to make the correct spelling choice. Point out that we require an **ear** in order to <u>h**ear**</u> something. In addition, make sure that students understand the role of the *mute e* in converting **her** to **her<u>e</u>** (see p.67).

With regard to the 4 sets of *Paired Words* below, emphasise to students that the words **sound** different. Don't be surprised if your students struggle with these words. It may take several lessons before confusion in this area is reduced or eradicated.

off / of

The tendency here is for students to write **of** when attempting to spell **off**. Emphasise that these words *sound* different: **of** sounds like **ov** but English words never end with 'v'. When students hear the **f** in **off** they need to exaggerate the sound with a double **ff**.

were / where

Confusion between these two words has proved to be almost universal among students with weak literacy skills. With regular practice, however, the following mnemonic has proved extremely effective. Ask students to imagine the **h** in w**h**ere as the profile of a dining room chair: when spelling **where**, students should be encouraged to repeat the words **"w**h**ere – chair"** so that the rhyme indicates the need to include the *chair* (**h**). Similarly, when spelling **were**, encourage students to think about **"were - chair"**. When students don't hear the rhyme, they need to leave the **h** out. Note that the *'Question Word Rule'* also applies here (see Golden Rules overleaf).

who / how

As is the case with *were/where*, confusion between these two words occurs time and again. Firstly, warn your student to avoid spelling h<u>ow</u> as h<u>aw.</u> This is an extremely common mistake. An even more likely error, however, is for students to write **how** when they intend to spell **who**. A useful mnemonic is: '**who** <u>w</u>ill <u>h</u>ave <u>o</u>ranges?' Ask the student to practise writing **who** whilst repeating this phrase. When repeating the word **who**, we recommend that students simultaneously tap the table with a pen in order to avoid beginning with a **h** (i.e. **hwho**): e.g. student repeats: '**who** (tap) <u>w</u>ill <u>h</u>ave <u>o</u>ranges?'

know / now

The tendency here is for **know** to be incorrectly spelt as **now**.
To deal with this problem, encourage students to do the following:
a) When writing **know**, repeat the sentence *'I **know** the **K**ing'*.
     As this makes sense, **k** for <u>k</u>ing is to be included (<u>k</u>**now**).
b) When writing **now**, repeat the sentence *' I **now** the King '*.
     As this - of course - does <u>not</u> make sense, **k** for <u>k</u>ing is to be excluded (- **now**).

GOLDEN RULES

For people with literacy problems, the complexity and inconsistency of the English language means that rules for spelling are of limited value. In simple terms, there are just too many alternative ways of spelling particular sounds. Consider for instance the following sentence:

One of these people on the quay seized the key to the green bathing machine and gave it to the chief officer who threw it in the sea. *

This sentence contains up to nine ways of spelling the 'ee' sound. For those with difficulties in processing and recalling symbolic information, there are no rules or teaching methods which will be particularly helpful. Even if a student were to learn all the alternative ways of spelling ' ee ' - no mean feat in itself - there are no mechanisms nor rules to allow them to make the correct spelling choice. Indeed, severely dyslexic students are often unable to decide with confidence between two alternatives (for example, whether to write *sownd* or *sound*).

In addition, due to weaknesses in both short term and sequential memory, dyslexic students find it very difficult to remember rules and/or to apply them to particular words in the context of their writing. Thus, our aim is not to teach rules for spelling which are inconsistent and very difficult to recall but to ensure that our students can read and spell the most used words in the English language with accuracy and confidence (**see 'Why Spelling Does Matter' page 6**).

Having said all of the above, there are certain 'golden rules' that do help students to deal with high frequency words. Students should be reminded of these regularly - particularly when the relevant words are being analysed during a spelling lesson. Again, don't expect your students to remember these rules quickly and easily: plenty of repetition and practice is required before students can internalise these principles and apply them to their reading and spelling.

1. Question Words

Tell your students that this term refers to words that can be used on their own to ask a question. For example : *what?, when?, which?, why?* and *where?*

Note that in each case, the **bold** letter **h** is silent. Impress upon your students that Question Words require a silent **h**. Reinforce this point by contrasting *when / went* and *which / with*. The two exceptions to this rule among our target words (i.e. *while* and *white*) should be dealt with as and when they arise.

* Quotation from Dyslexia or Illiteracy? Peter Young and Colin Tyre. Copyright © 1983 The Open University Press.

2. Double Consonants

The rule for double consonants should only be used as a guide to help in spelling high frequency words. Where the rule applies, it certainly helps to point it out. Unfortunately, however, there are far too many exceptions for it to be applied with confidence to other words.

To illustrate the rule, point out how the addition of a second **n** to the word **diner** to form **dinner** changes the preceding vowel from a long **i** (e.g. *wine*) to a short **i** (e.g. *win*).
The same principle applies to **filed** and **filled** or to **noble** and **nobble**.

This rule is particularly useful when we need to add *...ing* to a verb: for example, a double consonant gives us *hopping* rather than *hoping* or *scrapping* rather than *scraping.*

3. 'b' and 'd' confusion

Most people who have spent time teaching students with weak literacy skills will be aware that confusion between **b** and **d** is extremely common. This can manifest itself in both reading and spelling. Unlike **p** and **q** for example, **b** and **d** creates both visual and auditory confusion and there are no simple solutions. In our experience, the best approach is to encourage students to attempt *b* by writing *bat* before *ball*:-
(e.g. *l o - lo - b*). Similarly, ask students to attempt *d* by drawing a *dish* first (e.g. *o l - ol - d*).

4. Mute ' e ' Rule

Also known as the 'magic e', this rule tends to be grasped by people without literacy problems with little or no conscious effort. Nevertheless, it remains very important. Point out that generally, the addition of the 'mute e' changes the preceding vowel from a *short* to a *long* sound. For example, ask your student to note the change in the vowel sound as *rat* becomes *rate* and *pin* becomes *pine.* Of course, the **'e'** itself remains silent.

5. Regional Variations

Obviously, regional accents make a difference to the way certain words are pronounced. Tutors need to bear this in mind as variations in the *sound* of words may make a difference to the way they are spelt. For instance, in Yorkshire, *hard* vowel sounds tend to predominate which may produce a different sort of spelling error from those which are evident in certain parts of the south of England: e.g. *path / parth* and *bath / barth.* This is not a major problem but tutors need to be aware of it particularly when demonstrating the relevant phonetic spellings.

<table>
<tr><td colspan="2">WORD GUIDE</td><td>Most Used Words 1-50 Guide</td></tr>
<tr><td></td><td>Phonic Alternatives
& Common Errors</td><td>Tips for Word Analysis and Mnemonics (memory aids)</td></tr>
<tr><td>1 all</td><td>oll</td><td></td></tr>
<tr><td>2 an</td><td></td><td></td></tr>
<tr><td>3 and</td><td></td><td></td></tr>
<tr><td>4 are</td><td>ar / or</td><td>When combined with other letters (eg. bar, car) the 'e' is dropped.</td></tr>
<tr><td>5 as</td><td>az</td><td></td></tr>
<tr><td>6 at</td><td></td><td></td></tr>
<tr><td>7 be</td><td>by /bee</td><td>Compare and contrast with by.</td></tr>
<tr><td>8 but</td><td></td><td></td></tr>
<tr><td>9 by</td><td>biy / buy / bye</td><td>y says i : we <u>never</u> see iy.</td></tr>
<tr><td>10 came</td><td>come / caim / kame</td><td></td></tr>
<tr><td>11 can</td><td></td><td></td></tr>
<tr><td>12 do</td><td>du / doo / duw</td><td></td></tr>
<tr><td>13 each</td><td>ech / eech</td><td>Point out that there are many ways to spell ee.</td></tr>
<tr><td>14 from</td><td>form</td><td>Note the tendency to transpose letters (ro / or).</td></tr>
<tr><td>15 had</td><td></td><td></td></tr>
<tr><td>16 have</td><td>hav</td><td>Words never end with v : hence the 'e'.</td></tr>
<tr><td>17 he</td><td>hee</td><td></td></tr>
<tr><td>18 his</td><td>hiz</td><td></td></tr>
<tr><td>19 I</td><td>eye</td><td></td></tr>
<tr><td>20 if</td><td>iff</td><td></td></tr>
<tr><td>21 in</td><td></td><td></td></tr>
<tr><td>22 is</td><td>iz</td><td></td></tr>
</table>

Paired Words have their own section in the Teaching Guide (see pages 64-65).

During the Analysis step of the **RAWS** process demonstrate on paper the relevant phonetic spelling. Our basic approach is to pre-empt the mistakes which are most likely to occur. Experience will enable tutors to point out likely errors beforehand.

	Phonic Alternatives & Common Errors	Tips for Word Analysis and Mnemonics (memory aids)
23 **it**		
24 **not**	knot	
25 **on**	no	
26 **one**	wun / won	This spelling applies to the number only.
27 **or**	ore / are / our	
28 **said**	sed	<u>s</u>aid <u>a</u>n <u>i</u>nteresting <u>d</u>octor.
29 **she**	shee	
30 **that**	theat	**th** can say **the** even without an **e**.
31 **the**	th	
32 **they**	thay	To avoid **thay** students should write **the** first.
33 **this**	theis / these	Compare and contrast with **these**.
34 **to**	tu / too	Try to provide examples to avoid confusion with **too**.
35 **use**	youse / yous	Avoid starting with **you** : we need the long vowel **u**. Compare and contrast with **us**.
36 **was**	woz / wos	**wa** usually says **wo**.
37 **we**	wee	
38 **what**	wot / wat	A question word requires a silent **h** : **wa** usually says **wo** (p.66).
39 **when**	wen	A question word requires a silent **h** : contrast **went** (p.66).
40 **which**	witch / wich	A question word requires a silent **h** : contrast **with** (p.66).
41 **with**	whith	Not a question word : contrast **which** (p.66).
42 **word**	werd / wurd	**or** says **er** as in w**or**k and w**or**ld.
43 **you**	yuw / yoo	
44 **your**	yore / yor	y - - r : your <u>o</u>range <u>u</u>mbrella.

Mnemonics (also known as 'memory aids') have proven themselves to be invaluable in helping students to spell accurately. Don't expect your student to remember and apply these mnemonics immediately - weaknesses in both short-term memory and sequencing make this difficult - but, once stored in long-term memory, they will prove very useful.

	Phonic Alternatives & Common Errors	Tips for Word Analysis and Mnemonics (memory aids)
51 **about**	abowt / adout	b/d confusion: **b**at before **b**all (p.67).
52 **been**	bean / bene	The **an** in bean indicates a **can** of beans.
53 **call**	coll	
54 **come**	cum	Point out the phonetic similarity to **some**.
55 **could**	cud	c- - - d: **c**ould **o**range **u**mbrellas **l**eak.
56 **day**	daye	**ay** always has a long sound. No mute **e** required.
57 **did**		
58 **down**	doun / bown	b/d confusion: **d**og's **d**ish comes first (p.67).
59 **find**	fined / finde	...**ind** requires a long vowel (m**ind**, k**ind** etc.).
60 **first**	frist	To avoid f**ri**st: I come f**ir**st.
61 **get**		
62 **go**	gow	
63 **has**	haz	
64 **her**	hur / here	
65 **him**	hem	
66 **into**	intu	
67 **like**	lice / lick	**e** makes **c** say **s** (lice): hence the need for **k**.
68 **long**		
69 **look**	luck	**oo** represents two eyes in order to look.
70 **made**	maid / mayd	
71 **make**	mace / mack	**e** makes **c** say **s** (mace): hence the need for **k**.
72 **many**	meny	**m**any **a**nts **n**eed **y**oghurt.
73 **may**	maye / my	**ay** always has a long sound. No mute **e** required.
74 **more**	moor / mour	Compare and contrast with **moor**.

Remember to demonstrate the relevant phonetic spellings on paper.

	Phonic Alternatives & Common Errors	Tips for Word Analysis and Mnemonics (memory aids)
75 **my**	miy / may	**y** says **i**: we <u>never</u> see **iy**.
76 **no**	now / on	
77 **now**	naw	Point out that **aw** never says **ow**.
78 **number**	numder	Write **b** with **b**at before **b**all (p.67).
79 **oil**	oyl / ole	
80 **other**	uther / outher / over	Take care with pronunciation to avoid confusion with **over**.
81 **out**	owt / awt	
82 **over**	other	Take care with pronunciation to avoid confusion with **other**.
83 **part**		
84 **people**	peepul	<u>p</u>eople <u>e</u>at <u>o</u>ranges <u>p</u>eople <u>l</u>ike <u>e</u>ating.
85 **see**	sea	**ee** represents two eyes in order to s**ee**.
86 **so**	sow	
87 **some**	sum	Point out the phonetic similarity to **come**.
88 **than**	thean	**th** can say **the** even without an **e**.
89 **them**		
90 **then**		
91 **these**	thees / theas / this	Compare and contrast with **this** and point out that there are many ways to spell **ee**.
92 **time**		
93 **two**	tow / to / too	To avoid **tow** think about <u>t</u>wo <u>w</u>heels <u>o</u>n.
94 **up**		
95 **water**	worter / warter	**wa** usually says **wo**.
96 **way**	waye / why	**ay** always has a long **a** sound. No mute **e** required.
97 **will**	whill / well	
98 **would**	wud / wood	w- - - d: **w**ould **o**range **u**mbrellas **l**eak.

Use the mnemonics where appropriate.

	Phonic Alternatives & Common Errors	Tips for Word Analysis and Mnemonics (memory aids)
101 **after**		
102 **also**	allso / alsow	Contrast the beginning of words (**al**most, **al**ready) with the end (b**all**, c**all**). This **al**ways happens.
103 **any**	eny	Point out the phonetic similarity with m**any**.
104 **around**	arownd / arond	Use the orange **umbrella** to avoid arownd.
105 **back**		
106 **before**	befor / befour	**b**efore **e**ating **f**ood **o**ld **R**onnie **e**xercises.
107 **boy**		
108 **follow**	folow	Note the rule for double consonants (page 67).
109 **form**	from	Note the tendency to transpose letters (**or/ro**).
110 **give**	giv	Words never end with **v**: hence the 'e'.
111 **good**	gud	Point out that **oo** often says **u**.
112 **great**	grate / grait	It is gr**eat** to **eat**.
113 **help**		
114 **just**	gust	Point out that **g** only says **j** when followed by **e** or **i**.
115 **line**		
116 **little**	littel / litle / littul	...**le** always says **ul**. Note the rule for double consonants (page 67).
117 **live**	liv	Words never end with **v**: hence the 'e'.
118 **man**		
119 **me**	mee	
120 **mean**	meen / mene	Point out that there are many ways to spell **ee**.
121 **most**	moste / must	
122 **much**	mutch	
123 **name**	naim	
124 **new**	nuw / knew	**ew** often says you.

Remember to demonstrate the relevant phonetic spellings on paper.

	Phonic Alternatives & Common Errors	Tips for Word Analysis and Mnemonics (memory aids)
125 **old**	owld	
126 **only**	onley / onely / ownly	…**ley** applies to a name or place (Brad**ley**, Ship**ley**).
127 **our**	ower / are / or	To avoid **ower**: **our o̲range u̲mbrella**.
128 **place**	plaice / plays	**e** makes **c** say **s**: pla**ce**.
129 **same**	saim	
130 **say**	saye	**ay** always has a long **a** sound. No mute **e** required.
131 **sentence**	sentens / sentance	**e** makes **c** say **s**: senten**ce**.
132 **set**		
133 **show**		
134 **small**	smoll	Note the importance of avoiding o̲ll.
135 **sound**	sownd / sond	Use the o̲range u̲mbrella to avoid sownd.
136 **take**	tace / tack	**e** makes **c** say **s** (ta**ce**): hence the need for **k**.
137 **tell**	tel	
138 **thing**	think	
139 **think**	thing	
140 **three**		
141 **through**	threw / throught	thr - - - - : followed by o̲range u̲nder g̲reen h̲edge.
142 **too**	two / to	Try to provide examples to avoid confusion with **to**.
143 **very**	verry	
144 **want**	wont / what	**wa** usually says **wo**.
145 **work**	werk	**or** says **er** as in w**or**d and w**or**ld.
146 **year**	yeer / yere	

Use the mnemonics where appropriate.

	Phonic Alternatives & Common Errors	**Tips for Word Analysis and Mnemonics (memory aids)**
151 **again**	agane / agen	Note alternative pronunciation: ag**a**ne & ag**e**n.
152 **air**	are	
153 **animal**	animul / aminal	
154 **another**	anuther / anouther	Stress the importance of **other** (e.g. br**other**, m**other**).
155 **answer**	anser / ansewr	Ask your student to spot the silent letter: ans<u>w</u>er.
156 **ask**	asck	
157 **away**		
158 **because**	becos / becouse	<u>b</u>irds <u>e</u>at <u>c</u>rumbs <u>a</u>fter <u>u</u>ncle <u>s</u>tops <u>e</u>ating. <u>b</u>ecause <u>e</u>lephants <u>c</u>an't <u>a</u>nswer <u>u</u>s <u>s</u>aid <u>e</u>mma.
159 **big**		
160 **change**	chanje / chang	**e** makes **g** say **j**: chang**e**.
161 **different**	diferent / difrent diffrent	Note the rule for double consonants (page 67).
162 **does**	dus / dose	<u>d</u>oes <u>o</u>liver <u>e</u>at <u>s</u>ausages.
163 **end**		
164 **England**	Ingland / Eingland	
165 **even**	evan	
166 **found**	fownd / fond	Use the <u>o</u>range <u>u</u>mbrella to avoid fownd.
167 **hand**		
168 **high**	hi	Ask your student to identify the silent letters: hi<u>gh</u>.
169 **home**		
170 **house**	howse / houes	
171 **kind**	kinde / cind	**i** makes **c** say **s** (**c**ind): hence the need for **k**.
172 **land**		
173 **large**	larg / largh / lager	**e** makes **g** say **j**: larg**e**.
174 **learn**	lern / lurn	**ear** can say **er** (e.g. h**ear**d, **ear**th).
175 **letter**	leter	Note the rule for double consonants (page 67).

	Phonic Alternatives & Common Errors	Tips for Word Analysis and Mnemonics (memory aids)
176 **listen**	lissen	Note the silent 't'.
177 **men**		
178 **mother**	muther / mouther	Stress the importance of **other** (e.g. br**other**, an**other**).
179 **move**		
180 **must**	most	
181 **need**	nead / nede / knead	Point out that there are many ways to spell **ee**.
182 **page**	paje / paige	**e** makes **g** say **j**: pa**ge**.
183 **picture**	picktur / picher	
184 **play**		
185 **point**	poynt / pont	
186 **put**		
187 **read**	reed / rede	Point out that there are many ways to spell **ee**.
188 **should**	shud	**sh**- - - **d**: **sh**ould **o**range **u**mbrellas **l**eak.
189 **spell**		
190 **still**	stil	
191 **study**	studdy / studey	
192 **such**	sutch / soch	
193 **try**	triy / trie	**y** says **i**: we <u>never</u> see **iy**.
194 **turn**	tern / trun	To avoid tern, think about a **U** t**urn**.
195 **us**	uz / use	Compare and contrast with **use**.
196 **well**		
197 **went**	whent	Not a question word: contrast **when** (p.66).
198 **why**	wiy / way	A question word: **y** says **i**: we <u>never</u> see **iy**.
199 **world**	werld / word / would	**or** says **er** as in w**or**d and w**or**k.

	Phonic Alternatives & Common Errors	**Tips for Word Analysis and Mnemonics (memory aids)**
201 **add**		
202 **along**		
203 **always**	allways	Contrast the beginning of words (**almost**, **already**) with the end (**ball**, **call**). This **alw**ays happens.
204 **begin**	bigin / begain	Compare and contrast with begun and began.
205 **below**	bellow	
206 **between**	betwean / betwene	
207 **both**	bothe	
208 **city**	sity / citie	**i** makes **c** say **s**: city.
209 **close**	cloes / clothes	
210 **country**	cuntry / county	Ask your student to spot the silent letter: c<u>o</u>untry.
211 **don't**	downt / do'nt	The apostrophe represents a missing letter (do n<u>o</u>t).
212 **earth**	erth	Emphasise that there are many ways to spell **er**. **ear** can say **er** (e.g. **learn**, **heard**).
213 **every**	evry	Emphasise the **bold** letter: ev<u>e</u>ry.
214 **example**	egsampul	…**le** always says **ul**. Beware of the abbreviation **eg**.
215 **eye**	eiy / eya	**y** is saying **i**.
216 **father**	farther	
217 **few**	fuw / phew	Point out that **ew** often says **you** (new, stew…).
218 **food**	fude	
219 **got**		
220 **group**	groop	Use the <u>o</u>range <u>u</u>mbrella to avoid groop.
221 **hard**	hared	When combined with other letters (e.g. **bar**, **car**) the 'e' in are is dropped.
222 **head**	hed	
223 **important**	inportant / importent	Emphasise the **bold** letters: i<u>m</u>port<u>a</u>nt.
224 **keep**	ceep / keap	**e** makes **c** say **s** (ceep) : hence the need for **k**.
225 **last**		

	Phonic Alternatives & Common Errors	Tips for Word Analysis and Mnemonics (memory aids)
226 **left**		
227 **life**	live	
228 **light**	lite	l - - - - : <u>i</u>diots <u>g</u>ulp <u>h</u>ot <u>t</u>ea.
229 **might**	mite	m - - - -: <u>i</u>diots <u>g</u>ulp <u>h</u>ot <u>t</u>ea.
230 **near**	neer / nere	
231 **never**	neaver / nether	
232 **next**	nexst	
233 **often**	oftun / offen	Emphasise the **bold** letters: of**te**n. Note the alternative pronunciations: oftun & offen.
234 **open**		
235 **own**	oan / owen	
236 **paper**		
237 **plant**		
238 **run**		
239 **saw**	sore / so	To avoid **sore / so** : I <u>saw</u> <u>**a**</u> <u>w</u>asp.
240 **school**	skool	**ch** sometimes says **k**.
241 **seem**	seam / seme	To avoid **seam**: it s**ee**ms I can s**ee**.
242 **something**	sumthing / somthing	
243 **start**		
244 **story**	storey	
245 **those**	thoes / thoughs	
246 **thought**	thort / thorught / throught	th - - - - t: <u>o</u>range <u>u</u>nder <u>g</u>reen <u>h</u>edge.
247 **together**	tugether / togher	
248 **tree**		
249 **under**		
250 **while**	wile	Ask your student to identify the silent letter: w<u>h</u>ile. An exception to the rule - it is <u>not</u> a question word.

		Phonic Alternatives & Common Errors	Tips for Word Analysis and Mnemonics (memory aids)
251	**above**	abuv	**ove** says **uv**: (e.g. **love**, **dove**).
252	**almost**	allmost	Contrast the beginning of words (**also**, **already**) with the end (**ball**, **call**). This **al**ways happens.
253	**began**	bigan / begain	Compare and contrast with begun and begin.
254	**body**	boddy	
255	**book**	buck	**oo** can say **u** as in st**oo**d.
256	**car**	care	
257	**carry**	carrie / cary	Note the rule for double consonants (page 67).
258	**children**	childern	Note the tendency to transpose letters (**re** /**er**).
259	**colour**	culler / color	At the end of a word, ...**our** often says ...**er**.
260	**cut**	kut	
261	**eat**	eet / ete	Point out that there are many ways to spell '**ee**'.
262	**enough**	inuff / enought	en- - - -: **o**range **u**nder **g**reen **h**edge.
263	**Europe**	urop / yourup	
264	**face**	fase	**e** makes **c** say **s**: **face**.
265	**family**	famliy	**y** says **i**: we <u>never</u> see **iy**.
266	**far**	fare	When combined with other letters (e.g. **bar**, **car**) the **e** in **ar<u>e</u>** is dropped.
267	**feel**	feal / fele	Point out that there are many ways to spell '**ee**'.
268	**feet**	feat / fete	Point out that there are many ways to spell '**ee**'.
269	**final**	finel / finul	To avoid finel, emphasise the **bold** letter: fin**a**l.
270	**girl**	gril	Note the tendency to transpose letters (**ir** /**ri**).
271	**grow**	gro	
272	**heat**	heet / hete	Point out that there are many ways to spell '**ee**'.
273	**idea**	idear / ideer	
274	**late**	lait	
275	**leave**	leve / leav	Words never end with **v**. Emphasise the **bold** letters: **l**ea**v**e.

		Phonic Alternatives & Common Errors	Tips for Word Analysis and Mnemonics (memory aids)
276	**list**		
277	**mile**		
278	**miss**	mis	
279	**mountain**	mounten / mountian	Emphasise the **bold** letters : m**ountai**n.
280	**music**	musik	
281	**night**	nite / knight	n- - - -: <u>i</u>diots <u>g</u>ulp <u>h</u>ot <u>t</u>ea.
282	**once**	wuns / onec	**e** makes **c** say **s**: on**ce**. Avoid starting with **one**.
283	**real**	reel / rele	Point out that there are many ways to spell 'ee'.
284	**river**		
285	**sea**	see	Compare and contrast with **see**.
286	**second**	seckond	
287	**side**	sighed	
288	**sometimes**	sumtimes / somtimes	
289	**song**		
290	**soon**	sune / sone	
291	**state**	stayt	
292	**stop**		
293	**talk**	tork	**alk** says **ork**: (e.g. w**alk**, ch**alk**).
294	**took**	tuck	**oo** can say **u** as in g**oo**d.
295	**until**	untill / untile	
296	**walk**	work / wark	**alk** says **ork**: (e.g. t**alk**, ch**alk**).
297	**watch**	wotch / whatch	Not a question word: contrast w**hat** (p.66).
298	**white**	wite / wight	Ask your student to identify the silent letter : w<u>h</u>ite. An exception to the rule - it is <u>not</u> a question word.
299	**without**	whithout	Not a question word: contrast w**hich** (p.66).
300	**young**	yung	Ask your student to spot the silent letter: y<u>o</u>ung.

A series of videos runs in conjunction with this lesson guide: **www.toe-by-toe.co.uk**

---

*Before starting Test 1 you should study the **SUS3** reading technique on pages 30-31.*

Test 1
- Sentence dictation for MUW 1-50 (Page18).
- SUS3 reading MUW 1-50 (P32).

Test 2
- Spelling List Test MUW 1-50 (P39).
- SUS3 reading MUW 1-50 (P32).

Tutors only: after the lesson, tutors need to:-
- *Transfer the negatives from MUW 1-50 List Test (P39) to the Control Page (P53).*
- *Underline the errors in sentences (P18) and transfer any <u>additional</u> negatives to the Control Page (P53).*

If there are fewer than 8 negatives on the Control Page from this point on follow LESSON GUIDE B (page 82)

LESSON GUIDE A covers the *MUW* in blocks of 50 words. It is designed for weaker students with severe spelling problems who tend to make a lot of errors when tested.

---

*Before starting Lesson 1 study the **RAWS** spelling process on pages 42-45.*

Lesson 1
- *Tutors choose 8 negatives from the Control Page (P53) and write them on Row A of a RAWS spelling form. Copy the same words onto the first Spelling Dictation Box (P46). Prepare for RAWS by consulting the Word Guide and the Golden Rules (P66-69).*
- SUS3 reading MUW 1-50 - if necessary (P32).
- Follow the first RAWS process.

Lesson 2
- Complete RAWS process (P52 C).
- SUS3 reading MUW 1-50 - if necessary (P32).
- *Tutors: choose 8 negatives from the Control Page (P53) and write them on a RAWS form and a dictation box (P46). Use the Word Guide.*
- Follow the second RAWS process.

Lesson 3

- From the Control Page (P.53) ask students to spell the positives (words which were ticked on the previous test) on paper. Mark with a tick or a dot.
- Complete the RAWS process (P52C).
- SUS3 reading MUW 1-50 if necessary (P32).
- *Tutors: choose 8 negatives from the Control Page (P53) and write them on a RAWS form and a dictation box (P46). Use the Word Guide.*
- Follow the third RAWS process.

Lesson 4

- Ask students to spell the positives from the Control Page (P.53) on paper.
- Complete the RAWS Process (P52C).
- Sentence dictation for MUW 51-100 (P20).

Lesson 5

- Tutors: choose 6 negatives from the Control Page (P53) plus 2 Paired Words (e.g. of/off) and write them on a RAWS form and a dictation box (P46). Before the lesson, study the Teaching Guide (P60-65) until you understand how to deal with Paired Words.
- Follow the fourth RAWS process.

Lesson 6

- Ask students to spell the positives from the Control Page (P.53) on paper.
- Complete the RAWS Process (P52C).
- SUS3 reading MUW 51-100 (P33).

Lesson 7

- Spelling List Test MUW 51-100 (P39).
- SUS3 reading MUW 51-100 (P33).

Tutors only: after the lesson, tutors need to:-

- Transfer the negatives from MUW 51-100 List Test (P39) to the Control Page (P54).
- Underline the errors in sentences (P20) and transfer any <u>additional</u> negatives to the Control Page (P54).

Lesson 8

- SUS3 reading MUW 51-100 if necessary (P33).
- *Tutors: choose 6 negatives from the Control Page (P53-54) plus 2 Paired Words and write them on a RAWS form and a dictation box (P46). Use the word guide.*
- Follow the 5th RAWS process.

From this point on, try to alternate lessons between following the RAWS process and a marking lesson, with at least 24 hours in between.

LESSON GUIDE B covers the *MUW* in blocks of 100 words. It is suitable for stronger students who make fewer errors.

Lesson 1
- Sentence dictation for MUW 51-100 (P20).
- SUS3 reading MUW 1-100 (P32-33).

Lesson 2
- Spelling List Test MUW 51-100 (P39).
- SUS3 reading 1-100 (P32-33).

Tutors only: after the lesson, tutors need to:-
- *Transfer the negatives from MUW 1-100 List Test (P39) to the Control Page (P53-54).*
- *Underline the errors in sentences (P18/20) and transfer any <u>additional </u>negatives to the Control Page (P53-54).*

*Before starting Lesson 3 study the **RAWS** spelling process on pages 42-45.*

Lesson 3
- *Tutors choose 8 negatives from the Control Page (P53-54) and write them on Row A of a RAWS spelling form. Copy the same words onto the first Spelling Dictation Box (P46). Prepare for RAWS by consulting the Word Guide and the Golden Rules (P66-71).*
- *SUS3 reading MUW 1-100 necessary (P32-33).*
- *Follow the first RAWS process.*

Lesson 4
- *Complete RAWS process (P52 C).*
- *SUS3 reading MUW 1-100 - if necessary (P32-33).*
- *Tutors: choose 8 negatives from the Control Page (P53-54) and write them on a RAWS form and a dictation box (P46). Use the Word Guide.*
- *Follow the second RAWS process.*

Lesson 5
- From the Control Page (P.53-54) ask students to spell the positives (words which were ticked on the previous test) on paper. Mark with a tick or a dot.
- *Complete RAWS process (P52C).*
- *SUS3 reading MUW 1-100 - if necessary (P32-33).*
- *Tutors: choose 8 negatives from the Control Page (P53-54) and write them on a RAWS form and a dictation box (P46). Use the Word Guide.*
- *Follow the third RAWS process.*

Lesson 6

- Ask students to spell the positives from the Control Page (P.53-54) on paper.
- *Complete RAWS process (P52C).*
- *Sentence dictation for MUW 101-150 (P22).*

Lesson 7

- *Tutors: choose 6 negatives from the Control Page (P53-54) plus 2 Paired Words (e.g. of/off) and write them on a RAWS form and a dictation box (P46). Before the lesson, study the Teaching Guide (P60-65) until you understand how to deal with Paired Words.*
- Follow the fourth RAWS process.

Lesson 8

- Ask students to spell the positives from the Control Page (P.53-54) on paper.
- Complete RAWS process (P52C).
- SUS3 reading MUW 1-150 (P32-34).

Lesson 9

- Spelling List Test 101-150 (P40).
- SUS3 reading MUW 1-150 (P32-34).

Lesson 10

- Sentence dictation for MUW 151-200 (P24).
- SUS3 reading 1-200 (P32-35).

From this point on, try to alternate lessons between following the RAWS process and a marking lesson, with at least 24 hours in between.

OPTIONAL DIAGNOSTIC TEST

The sentences below contain a selection of the 300 most used words. The tutor should dictate them for students to write on lined paper. They have been carefully constructed with repetition of those words which commonly cause the most problems. The sentences are useful in two respects:-

1)   As a diagnostic tool to identify those students who will benefit from *Stareway To Spelling* and to highlight errors which can then be included in the RAWS process.

2)   As a final check - once the manual has been completed - which will identify any remaining negatives.

How do we learn to read and spell? It seems that some people do not have to try very hard. They could read and spell many of our words before they went off to school even if they did not work at home with their mother and father. When they look at a word, they can read it and also picture it so that when there was a need to write it down, they could do so. These people know that each word looks right.

For others, it is different. If they try to write a sentence, they know that we do not spell every word, the way that it sounds. ''You should know it by now'' they hear, but they don't.

Where to begin? Why does who sound like through? What on earth is the answer? It should be thought through once again but why would anyone want to? For example, think of important words like mountain, country, saw, while, colour and enough. Those are only a few examples, there are many more. You might know them at first but only until another day. Who are these people? They might have great new ideas which others may use but do not know the words we use most of all. But their work is important.

Who said 'together we can learn?' They were right. Now it is your turn. Watch us and listen as we use this book to learn to write and spell because it has almost all you will need.

STAREWAY TO SPELLING

RAWS Spelling Forms

Name : **Date :** ___ / ___ / ___   Row

A

B

C

D

E

F

Test Date   G

___ / ___ / ___

Name : **Date :** ___ / ___ / ___   Row

A

B

C

D

E

F

Test Date   G

___ / ___ / ___

STAREWAY TO SPELLING

RAWS Spelling Forms

Name :   **Date :** ___ / ___ / ___   **Row**

	Row
	A
	B
	C
	D
	E
	F
Test Date	G
___ / ___ / ___	

Name :   **Date :** ___ / ___ / ___   **Row**

	Row
	A
	B
	C
	D
	E
	F
Test Date	G
___ / ___ / ___	

Name :   Date : ____ / ____ / ____   Row

	Row
	A
	B
	C
	D
	E
	F
Test Date	G
____ / ____ / ____	

Name :   Date : ____ / ____ / ____   Row

	Row
	A
	B
	C
	D
	E
	F
Test Date	G
____ / ____ / ____	

Name :	Date : ___ / ___ / ___	Row
		A
		B
		C
		D
		E
		F
	Test Date	G
	___ / ___ / ___	

Name :	Date : ___ / ___ / ___	Row
		A
		B
		C
		D
		E
		F
	Test Date	G
	___ / ___ / ___	